Regina Noel

GIVE A LITTLE SNUGGLE

Illustrated by Mathew Havran

TEACUP PRESS

Thank you to my dear friend, Jonathan Campbell, for the music transcription. —Regina

Copyright © 2021 by Regina Noel

All rights reserved. Published in the United States by Teacup Press, an imprint of Fox Pointe Publishing, LLP. No part of this book may be reproduced in any form or by any electronic or mechanical means, including information storage and retrieval systems, without permission in writing from the publisher.

www.teacup-press.com • www.foxpointepublishing.com/author-regina-noel

Library of Congress Cataloging-in-Publication Data
Noel, Regina, author.
Eckman, Raven, editor.
Havran, Mathew, illustrator.
Hudson, Becca, designer.

Give a Little Snuggle / Regina Noel. – First edition.

Summary: An illustrated song for children, parents, and caregivers emphasizing the importance of physical touch in maintaining emotional health and growth.

ISBN 978-1-955743-51-8 (hardcover) / 978-1-952567-15-5 (softcover)
[1. Emotions & Feelings – Fiction. 2. Music – Fiction. 3. Family – Fiction. 4. Social Themes – Fiction. 5. Resilience – Fiction.]

Library of Congress Control Number: 2 0 2 1 9 0 2 8 0 8

Second printing - November 2025.

For Simone and Charles.
If you're muddled,
just ask me for a cuddle
and I'll give ya one.

To the Mamas, Papas, and Caregivers,

We find ourselves in the midst of a remarkable time in history. One that is both scary and exciting. The fear COVID-19 has elicited is warranted. Many of us are conflicted over the changing guidelines to keep safe: wear masks, social distance, and so on. As a global society, we've done our best. But, we really couldn't have anticipated the suffering that comes from the lack of physical contact, especially in children.

According to Virginia Satir, renowned family therapist, we need about 8 hugs a day for maintenance, and 12 for growth. The 20-second hug is your most powerful tool for calm and connectedness. It expresses empathy, compassion, love and care, and has the power to ease the most difficult of life's moments. Physiologically, hugging increases oxytocin (the love hormone), reduces blood pressure, and lowers cortisol (the stress hormone). For an extra boost of calm and connectedness, match your breathing to that of your "huggie." And count to 20 together.

Take your time.

Be fully present.

So, let's do our best to practice the CDC guidelines for our health and safety. At the same time, let's not overlook how crucial physical touch is, for our children especially. It may not be the time for snuggles with other relatives or friends——but it is always time for a snuggle within our immediate family/isolation group.

Here's to you——doing the best you can with what you've got.

And if you've got a snuggle in your heart, you've got more than you thought.

If you're feeling blue...

that just might see you through.

then a WIGGLE.

If you're muddled,

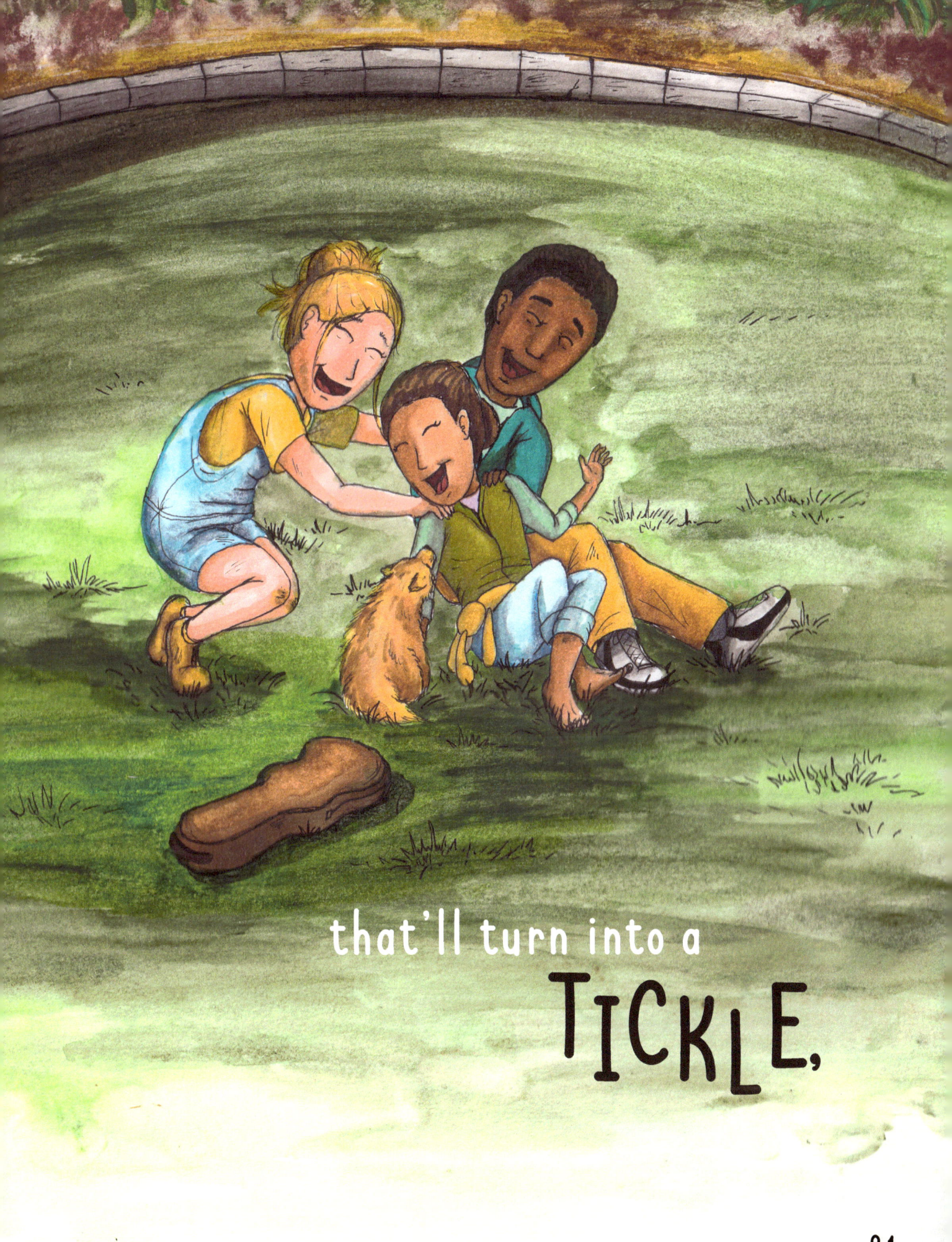

'cause
I love ya,
hon!

PLAY ALONG!

(Ukulele chords)

Meet The Creators...

Photo credit: Sara Stromseth-Troy

About The Author
Regina Noel

Regina Noel resides in Iowa with her two children and two dogs. She holds a BA in Music and Physical Education from Luther College, as well as an MA in Elementary Education from Grand Canyon University. Ms. Regina is the owner and instructor of the Regina Noel Music Studio, where she teaches private piano, voice, and ukulele lessons to children and adults of all ages and abilities. When she isn't teaching or writing, you can find Ms. Regina weight lifting, making music, making (and eating) chocolates, or just plain hanging out with her kiddos and doggos.

Photo credit: Brittany Todd

About The Illustrator
Mathew Havran

Mathew Havran of Decorah, Iowa is fairly new to the world of illustrating children's books, but not to drawing and painting. A self-taught artist since kindergarten, drawing quickly became his favorite pastime up into the present. Today, some of his other hobbies include playing the piano and ukulele, rollerblading, singing and beatboxing, and family-fun activities with his wife and two kids. He currently makes a living as a Test Technician at Collins Aerospace but has been devoting much of his free time to illustrating, painting, and muraling in his community. Much of his work can be seen around Decorah and on his Facebook page, "Artist Mathew Havran."

www.ingramcontent.com/pod-product-compliance
Lightning Source LLC
Chambersburg PA
CBHW042054050526
44107CB00109B/1132